The Last Supper

Poetic Journeys, Volume 3

Charles Harvey

Published by Wes Writers and Publishers, 2024.

While every precaution has been taken in the preparation of this book, the publisher assumes no responsibility for errors or omissions, or for damages resulting from the use of the information contained herein.

THE LAST SUPPER

First edition. March 9, 2024.

ISBN: 979-8224473885

Written by Charles Harvey.

Table of Contents

The Last Supper

by

Charles W. Harvey

PUBLISHED BY:

Wes Writer and Publishers

The Last Supper

Copyright © 2012 by Charles W. Harvey

Please subscribe to the mailing list for exciting updates. Thank you.
Subscribe[1]

Author's Website[2]

---

1. https://subscribepage.io/9sPXo5

2. http://charlesharveyauthor.wordpress.com/

About These Poems

Warning! Despite the title **The Last Supper**, these are not religious poems. These poems embrace at the intersection of the Sacred and the Profane. As all astute readers know, at that intersection lies the forbidden. These poems are forbidden to you if you are easily offended, if you read the lines but not between the lines. If you cannot embrace shades of gray, you will not like these poems. The author apologizes in advance for the lack of roses and limericks in these poems. These poems are not for children, little old ladies, or Church Mothers. However the church is in these poems.

You might get a whiff of the 80's in these verses. Ronald Reagan may be dead, but his legacy lives on. Nothing has changed much in corporate America. Greed rules. AIDS steals away our young men and women. The poem's title, The Last Supper, comes the mantra a young man recited as I fed him his last meal: A sip of water please/A little string beans/Wait now, you're rushing me.

If you love the Lord or the God in you, you will love these poems—not because they're religious, but because they strive to tell the truth.

Charles W. Harvey

1987 PEN/Southwest Discovery Prize Winner

****

BRUTUS

I want

love

love

love

so bad,

I am

thinking on

adopting

the coiled rattlesnake

that I saw

among the diamonds

and crucifixes

In Lucky's

Pawn Shop window.

Vanna's Image

Is it true

Vanna White

is selling her image?

Will she sell to me

some of her magic,

teach me to

turn my hair to honey,

and spin my sex

into oval rubies for men to mine?

When I look at her

will I turn to

a pillar of salt?

A Curse From God

"Father! Father!"

entreated the pie faced boy,

"I stretch my hands to thee."

Father looked down

upon the wormlike limbs

that rotted with gangrene.

He shook his head and

stuck out his tongue.

"Ha!

Thou suffer, because

thine mouth knew and suckled men

in their secret places.

Did you not hear your preacher?"

"Oh Father," Pie Face answered,

"I heard through grape vines

tea leaves, and bellicose

microphones all of your Ministers.

But when night cut off day

like an executioner's axe,

Your Minister's mouths sought mine.

Even you, Father,

put your mitre aside for me."

Father answered, "well lad

someone must pay the price

for my pleasure.You are

the chosen one.But I will

give you a prayer to offer me daily:

Lord. Lord. Fill this hollow bowl

of my belly with blood

So that I might give

an offering of thanks

for your mercy and grace

when I get to heaven.Amen.

Born Again

Well I knew the red bitch dog

wasn't what he needed, but I,

I always give my man what he wants.

Yes that's him driving that slut

named "Big Nina."He's getting

littler and littler 'cause he has

no food. You see

all of my money

went into buying him

that red bitch dog, "Big Nina."

We was on our way, yes we was

to the grocery store, when my man said,

"Baby, baby, a can of beans won't feed

what I wants fed. Take me to that car lot instead."

So I did.

I always give my man what he wants.

I knew he was in love with that red whore

when he patted her humped ass, when he

rubbed and rubbed himself against her tailight.

He said, "Myrtle, this will feed me."And so

I fed him to the whore, him and his intestines

packed with years of shit his Mama left in him—

pushed it up Big Nina's twat

with a hoe handle..

Now there he goes nestled in "Big Nina's" belly,

getting littler and littler, and she just a

swelling up all around him.

Soon and very soon,

he's going to be a skeleton.

When he dies for my sin

I want to sit his skull

on my bureau

and ask him to forgive me

for giving him what he wanted.

THE LAST SUPPER

"A sip of water please

A little string beans

Wait now, you're rushing me.

A sip of water please

A little rice

Just a little.

A little string beans

A sip of water please

A little more rice

Just a little bit

That's right.

Some string beans now

A sip of water please

Not too much.

That's right.

Some string beans

Some rice now.

Hold up. Hold up.

A sip of water please.

A little more string beans

Some rice

Just a little.

A sip of water please.

Hold up! Hold Up!

I got to rest now.

You're rushing me too fast."

LURKING LATE

A boy never lives

in your house.

It takes a man for that.

A boy lurks

in the late hour

on the lamplighted streets.

Home is where pussy can be sniffed

for the moment,

or where a ham sandwich is

consumed and forgotten.

His tennis shoes litter

the livingroom and a

pair of size 28 drawers

have to be untucked from

between couch cushions,

but the boy is not at home.

His heart, oh lord,

his heart roams.

DEAD TREES

Once they were the life,

dancing under twinkling balls

and wearing their best gold.

They hugged you like

a Queen embracing a leper

and you wanted to sniff their

most secret places, make them

sigh with your red tongue.

They were "cute"—

slender, chiseled, and muscled—

the color of coffee, the color of sand,

and if they had a dimple,

Lord, lord, say no more.

Now they are silent.

the eyes once lighted

are dimmed.They still come

to this place, pulled by

their lust to live

and hear the music, to not die.

In this place, where

they made their minor histories,

they stand to themselves

like old discarded props.

They have a new DJ

in this place

who in his dazzling white coat

and Bunsen Burners for eyes

calls out"Divas to the Dance Floor,"

but the divas are rooted

like old dead trees.

THE MAN...

is blood, teeth, tongue,

earwax, red shoes, fists,

war, asshole, penis, white drawers,

blue cap, damaged, naked, fucked up,

all together, all together fucked up

liver, onions, barbecue beer, white wine,

full of himself, hateful, trifling, industrious, humping all night,

elephant shooter, urine drinker, ball player,

ball licker, astronaut, astronut

cross burner, cross dresser, Martin Luther King,

Adolph Hitler, Adolph Caesar, Ghandi,

hair dresser, axe murderer, house painter,

President, dick sucker, Doctor,

cunt licker, toenail clippings, horse rider,

plane pilot, wife beater, Pope,

and devil, and misunderstood.

Always misunderstood.

The Oscars

And they go in and out

of your life like a movie.

What goes? Men go

in and out of your life

like a movie—men, like a movie

Rewind fast forward like a movie

men like a movie, in and out

of your life like a movie.

Like a what? like a Tom

like a Dick, like a Harry, like a Tyrone

Like a Tyrone again in and out

of your life men move

like a Dan, like a Fred,

like a George, like a Jose,

and like a, aw shit I forget his name.

Men move like a celluloid strip

fulla ghosts in and out of your life.

And they be action figures

And they be drama queens

dying slow deaths in the fast lane.

It takes two hours to live and die in the movies,

but it only takes a minute to fall in love

with a man that hates you the minute

he comes inside you.

Men move men move

in and out of your life.

I can't remember the names of movies anymore.

CAB DRIVER

I am without ears.

The appendages attached

to my head are

filled with fat.

I steer the cab

while a woman

peels scab after black scab

off your ass and soul

with her tongue dipped

in vinegar.

It is not my job to hear

confessions.

I just drive you to hell

and wonder will that woman tip.

SEVEN-THOUSAND AND ONE

I'm going to write me a book

and put you in it.

On the cover, it's you

all naked—black, brown, or red.

You will be bald, afroed, or dreadlocked.

Your sex will be nine inches of hot love

or six inches of sweet satisfaction.

Your ass will have more curve

than a sweet cantaloupe.

I'll title my book

"How To Love You."

From Genesis to Revelation

Every page will be blank.

All we have to do is fill them

one leaf at a time.

Don't worry the plot,

we make it up as we go along.

I wrote "the end" on page

Seven thousand and one.

So let's just take our time.

WHA'S UP

"Yo yo, wha's up

Yo yo, wha's up,"

boys chant—

gawky limbed, but

steeped in rhythm

feet going

tick tock tick tock

like a jazz clock

down my hall.

Levi's seat don't

hit the ass nowhere

except dragging

around the knees.

Pimples dot a smooth

oval face

eyes, bright black

and furtive

slender hands

stroke the Glock

nestled between

their thighs.

They spy me

on my knees

hands clasped

in furious prayer

to my all mighty father

maker of heaven

and black black dirt

my mouth is open

my tongue beats

a tune:

"Jesus, Jesus, Jesus!"

suddenly cold steel

touches my throat.

a trigger clicks,

rough hands squeeze

the back of my head.

I clutch thin hips,

look up and there

be Jesus, skinny

shaved head,

robed in gold.

My lord whispers,

"Yo, yo, wha's up."

THE OLD BLIND NIGGER

"Who is this

you got

all tied up

with barbed wire,

Captain?"

"It's the old blind nigger—

stepped into the women's

water closet."

"White women's?"

"Yep."

"Well I'll be damned.

You sure he's blind?"

"Don't know for sure.

Took his eyes out,

sent 'em to the FBI

lab in Washington."

"Well I hope he's not blind."

"Me too."

"Ain't no fun to kill

a blind nigger.

He can't see death a comin.'"

"Yep I like for a nigger

to see death—

watch 'em

shit out the greens

they done ate,

piss out the liquor

they done drank.

Remember Young Coon Bob?"

"Shur do.

Got so stanky

we had to give him

a kerosene bath.

He shur did holler!

Probably hadn't had a good bath

in all his sixteen years.

Didn't know what wet was."

"Yep."

"Well get on that 'puter

and see iffen they done

analyzed the Old Blind

Nigger's eyes."

"Yep he's blind allright.

FBI says eyes got as much

life as boiled eggs.

Hmph!"

"Damn!

Jesus don't intend for a white man

to get any joy today."

"Naw he don't.

Cuss his Jewish ass!"

"Maybe you can spit

in the dirt

and rub some mud

in them hollow sockets."

"I don't know, Brother Jake,

I just don't know.

POETRY ONLINE

A nigger screams

across a cotton field

under the moon tinted red

by twenty pairs of shimmering eyes

soaked in Cutty Sark and blood

.

"Goddamn, Jake! Don't drop

that Arab's kerosene!"

"You can have your son back, Aunty

when his balls are nice and crispy.

Gone back to church now."

A dead nigger's soul

is entered on the INTERNET"'s

scrolling pages.

Jake types

fingers soot black:

"Nigger flesh cooked

smells a lot like

Ol' Cal's Barbecue Hut

that squats behind

the ass of the Holiday Inn,

'cept Cal's Hut is

a lot quieter than

a burnin' nigger."

STRANGE BIRDS OF A FEATHER

They are foreigners to me—

these lipless people.

They remind me of

beakless birds.

But a bird wears a plumage

royally like a king.

These "foreigners" may

be kings of the moon

but they have no song

to sing to me.

Night

Jazz music plays

in the background

of nigger shadows

and niggers know this music

like they know rivers of blood

and the moon's-eye and the moon's-ass

glowing through car windows

sinking into the shadows of night sky.

In a room tainted with nigger shadows,

the bare floor swims with generations

splattered, shot dead as soon as

they catapult out of the penis

past hungry mouths.

And some generations wind up in ass holes

where shit and jazz get mixed up

by white boys who wish they were niggers

but the electric tanning bed is no substitute for

being a nigger. Even George Wallace

admitted he was lying when he stood brick wall

against the schoolhouse door.

He wanted to be touched by a nigger then.

Before he met St Peter

His old crippled body knew the joy

of nigger hands—hands steeped in jazz

and sweet love of nigger nights.

Night II

Nigger night—and jazz plays in

ethereal shadows that massage

pricks and the broken backs of white men

and generations get lost on

the street corners and in prisons.

Niggers touch prison where jazz

is metal and shank carving into ivory bone.

Dicks get thrust down throats.

A life sentence is a death sentence

any sentence spoken wrongly to the warden

even "Good morning." can get you the needle.

The nigger is on the street corner.

He cries for help, "Buy a piece of the rock.

    I just need tennis shoes.

    I'm only being prudential."

The nigger even touches the bourgeoisie sitting

in trendy cafes drinking tea laced with piss

be-bopping to jazz music, blue smoke, and ether.

Ether makes you sleep. The nigger is supposed

to make me sleep.

But he wakes me up

and kicks my ass out of bed.

I drift all day waiting

for the nigger to come again—

the nigger who will disappoint me,

who will expose my filth to the daylight.

And the Daylight will write

what a degenerate I am because I'm a nigger

and I am jazz

all the while wishing as his asshole tingles

he could be just like me.

THE LIBRARY

Eight-thirty and

the Library is

an odd place

to look for love.

Next to the toilets

I sit. I listen

to the bowls

belch obscenely

rude and loud as

they suck piss

and turds down

their narrow throats.

My throat is dry.

Lord, if I can't

be loved, please

make me a toilet

next time I cum

into your world.

College Life

The chapel bells and the boys

are such joys

for seeing eyes

I tingle at sights

I tingle at noise.

I love late night

moans and sighs.

I cannot say which

tingle tingles the most.

So let the boys make some joyful noise

and my heart sing happily.

BOOKS

The musty library sighs with

the sweet hum of sex.

Me, Auden, Langston, and Whitman

hear the soft jingle of belts unbuckling

and trousers gliding like silk

down thighs, past rough

scarred knees.

Dicks into asses go "slock slock"

like turds dropping

into toilets.

Beards scrape against cheek

sighs leap from hungry throats.

"Be quiet, Books!" whispers

the gnarled librarian.

Looking up from

the book of Leviticus.

POEM FOR A PAIR OF WHITE JEANS

Rise up! Rise up,

Lazarus!

Rise up and be

and sex me

and be here

for me. I need

your gifts of

muscles, melanin

cock, balls,

intellect, soul

guile, hope,

Man hoodness.

Rise up! Rise up,

Lazarus!

Rise up and be.

POETICS

Poems ought not have

extraneous noise.

Leave sound effects

for the drum, saxophone,

and tambourine.

Your words your words

are rhythm enough.

POETICS II

If you're "cute"

all of the womens

think your poems

are all good and

all of your

mediocrities

poetic verses

and manna.

    But I think

    your poems

    are bullshit.

NOTHING

No money

no honey

no love

no Mother

no Father

no sister

no brother

no aunty

no uncle

no christ

just an ASS—

me and

the one

who uses

mine.

STATE STREET, Chicago

Negroes buzz

in iron honeycombs

of bone, lust,

and murderous mortar.

These edifices lined

up like dominoes

wait for the finger

of God to set

the toppling in motion.

CHICAGO

is a brawler

punched drunk

lying on his ass

and sprawled over

white snow.

Niggas at his feet

white folks at the head

Mary Magdalene at his waist

beseeching,

"Lord, lord

there's gonna be a rumble

at the cross of State and Roosevelt."

THE DISTINGUISHED VISITOR

We open the side

of the Xerox Eight-Eighty

exposing the greased mechanical guts

as if offering a gift of entrails

to God.

Our visitor is a virile king of kings

of a dark starving nation.

Through the guts of the Eight-Eighty flows

red velvet paper like an issue of blood.

The king of virility is impressed

to the point of orgasm.

His tongues hang from between his lips

seek orifices, but protocol

keeps our pants up.

We offer donuts and tea.

The king and his entourage disperse

disappointed but full.

We throw away the red sheets

the eight-eighty has stamped with black ink.

We cut the power and the beast dies.

Dust dances down from heaven.

FUNKY BOY FINGERS

funky

funky

funky

boy fingers

funky

funky

funky

fingers

holding secret

funky

funky

scents

funky

funky

funky

boy fingers

funky

funky

funky

ass fingers

tasting

tasting

funky fingers

sucking

sucking

sucking

black boy

fingers

funky

funky

chicken eatin'

fingers

funky

funky

hot spicy

fingers

tonguing

tonguing

funky

nigga fingers

funky

funky

oh, Daddy!

funky

funky

funky

boy fingers.

GET OUT OF HEAVEN

OJ OJ OJ OJ

what time is your

lynching

gonna be?

TRIBES TRIBES TRIBES

of opaque ghosts are

coming for you, boy.

I hear them shout

from the red sky,

NIGGER GET OUT OF HEAVEN

before the sun goes

DOWN DOWN DOWN.

BARRIER

There is that

damned barrier.

———————————

I want I want

that sweet piece

of chocolate candy

with its tart

strawberry tongue,

but God with piercing

blue eyes keeps

me from my sweetness.

I wish chocolate candy

would let blue eyed

God alone.

Well who am I to

be chagrined?

I too wanted a taste

of blue eyed God

the other night.

Louisiana Casino Blues

I want with all my heart

to stand naked in front

of a black shirtless cum-filled

Louisiana jungle state trooper.

I want him to bark orders

at me," make me, make me, Mister Police,

spread my cheeks from Lake Charles

to the Foot of Canal Street."

He must dig into me with his baton

pull coins out of my ass

call me a boy, his candy ass nigger

though I am an old old man

with grandchildren older than his blood.

But it's just my luck

That I'll be roped

by some accordion playing

Cajun reserve deputy spitting

tobacco and lighting up

the black sky with crosses

and the glistening bodies of

naked niggers hanging

from weeping willows

just above the swamps.

BRICK SWEAT

"Chile, that nigguh so fine, he make a brick sweat!"

"What you say?"

"I say he so fine

he make a brick sweat."

"What you say again?"

"I say he is so fine

he makes a brick

sweet as sugar."

"He is fine, now."

"Yes he is."

"He is cinnamon."

"Oh yes he is."

"He is fine."

Yes he is."

He is black licorice."

"Oh that sweet sticky thing."

"I kissed him all."

"No you didn't!"

"Yes I did.I mopped his teeth

with my tongue.

I kissed him all

put one of his nipples

in his belly button."

"Lord, chile!"

"I kissed him

where the sun can't

reach, even when

he's naked on the

frying beach."

"Lord, chile."

"I loved him."

"Did you really?"

"I really.Pawned

a television that

was my Mama's."

"For him?"

"For him, baby

Bought him blue

lizard skin boots."

"From where?"

"From Neiman's"

"From where?"

"From Neiman's, I say."

Aw, chile, you don't know."

"Don't know what?"

"What love really is, baby."

"I loved him so much."

"How so much?"

"I went to the corner

and got him a ho'

when he didn't want me no more."

"Honey, that's love's love."

"Love's love,

That's what my man was."

"Why you say was?"

"I say was, 'cause he's gone."

"Gone where, baby?"

"Back to his wife."

"Aw, lord."

"But I ain't worried."

"Yeah don't worry."

A man grows on every street corner."

"That's the truth."

But you know?"

"Know what, girl?"

"A brick don't sweat

but one time in

your goddamn life.

And you better lick

while the sweating is good."

"Lord, lord, ain't that the truth."

PERHAPS

Perhaps we're just taking

up space in each other's empty

wounded, gushing hearts,

and bathing in blood so thick

our eyes turn

latenight red.

Perhaps you'll let me pull

down the straps of your sea blue

overallls and let my fingers crawl all over

your brown mountains and hills.

Perhaps the twin bed is just right for us.

Perhaps we will not annihilate

each other with tongues.

I want your lies, your smoke,

your children splattering the sheets,

my chest and chin.

Perhaps I'll let you bury me

and live on for twenty years

soaking your old bones

in my memories.

Doing Things Like That

Oh my God, George

look at all those coloreds

hanging around on the corner drinking

out of gold colored cans!

My stars! I've never seen the likes. Look

there's one with his hair tied up funny

like my dust mop and

smoking a teeny weeny cigarette and wobbling

and wobbling like he's got rubber legs.

Look, George, their pants are so low

I can see their little dark hinies.

What is our world coming to?

You never see us doing things like that,

like that, and that.

Yeah, lady, you right, we don't see you

doing stuff like that 'cause instead of gathering

at the perpendiculars of 125th and Lexington, Dowling and Elgin,

or any intersection of Hopeless Avenue and Despair Boulevard,

you people congregate like albino flies around water coolers in shimmering silver tombstones forty stories high.

You shoot up in supply closets using rubber bands

for tourniquets and paper clips for needles.

You people shake it and swing it in the men's room

eight times a day and get fat pockets

for doing it like that.

You hire secretaries wearing skirts hiked over their hips

(Look I can see their little dark bushes)

to bring you cups of pussy and make it legal

with w-2 forms.

You placate silly wife named Jill

with a quick two second "love ya, honey, bye."

and she thinks you don't love her any more

'cause you up to your ears in pie charts

while the truth be you got your nose in

Keisha's sweet potato pie.

You people spin spin spin lies about

niggas being five minutes late every day

while overlooking your own two hour lunches

to sneak off to see your therapists or abortionists

or combination of the two.

You hire strip-o-gram girls to dance on polished marble

boardroom table tops and write it off your taxes.

You people gather in cubicles and like

grinning chesire cats, you titter titter over black titties

ol' George has downloaded from the internet

and lick your thin lips while Leroy the token

grits his teeth and smiles through angry tears.

You cluck indignant over some black man accused of rape

while texting in your Blackberries—My Wife Wants it

    from a big black stud

    while I watch and

    my mouth waters

Yes you people be doing it High high on Main Street,

so much coke, it snows in July. But the firm

pays for your drug treatment programs conducted

in blue-walled fish tank soft lighted rooms

while poor nigguhs have their habits trotted

out on the six o'clock news, stamped on orange coveralls

and slammed against gray iron bars.

This is a tale of corporate culture

a few black tokens are permitted to tell.

We remain silent as shadows

while the poor white men "wounded"

by affirmative action box our ears

with lame jokes:

How's a nigger like a black jelly bean?

They both the last ones out the bag.

HAW HAW HAW HAW!

My wife said she wanted to be screwed by a black stud.

I brought her a horse. She told me to take it back.

It wasn't big enough. She wanted a black man.

HAW HAW HAW HAW!

And you you people be raping the whole world with a pencil—

buying stuff from Hong Kong at ten cents and selling the same shit

for a hundred dollars, and be manipulating the stock market

so that for every black man or poor white trash laid off

the market ejaculates ten points, and you issue nigguhs

credit cards to be used only at liquor stores at forty percent

on the almighty dollar for every forty ounce bought.

"My God, Jake, that's a brilliant idea—a million dollar bonus

for you and whose picture are we goin to put on the card,

MArtin Luther Koons?"

"Naw Naw, he's the old niggers hero. how 'bout one of them rappers,

Six Pack Shakur or Snoop Diggity Dog. Yeah that'll work.

And bring back the Chevy Novas for the niggers.

Yeah paint it red, green, and black. Trim the tires in gold.

Yeah niggers love gold. And we'll charge 'em 600 dollars a month

for twenty years.

Yeah, we can accept their college tuition as trade-in.

Now let's work on the Mexicans

God aren't they some hard workers?

One wetback works harder than ten niggers put together.

And here it is the 1999 lowrider Cadillac

Trimmed around the windows with that red fringe stuff.

HAW HAW HAW, Jake you're brilliant! You must be a Harvard Man!

Naw Iowa City Junior College class of '67.

HAW HAW HAW!

Excuse me, Mr. WonderBread, you have a call on line one.

Thanks Marge Ass, I mean Marge Ann.

Shhhh, okay did you knock off my wife?

What do you mean the bullet bounced off her forehead, man?

Now how the hell am I going to collect the insurance

and marry my secretary?

This is the last time I hire an Asian to do

any manual labor. You guys are real fuck ups.

So it goes on and on

until the five o'clock whistle

blows its shrill song

and Mr. Charlie and the tokens

ride their iron horses

to home and dinner cooked

in red, white, and blue

fried chicken boxes to watch TV shows

about themselves fucking themselves

until the valiums kick in

and induce dreams of rose petals

raining down from a shit colored sky

Ladies and gentleman, this message has been bought

to you by your friendly nigger lovers at Texaco

by the Anti Affirmative Action League of the United

Klu Klux Klan, by the KCBA (Keep Crack in Black America)

Division of the CIA, and now a message from Clarence Thomas:

"HAW HAW HAW

Who put this blonde pubic hair in my coke?"

'

POP TARTS AND TUNA

She was beautiful as

the lemon colored sun.

She wore her hair

in a blond bun.

She fed me pop tarts

and tuna.

We danced to Barry Manilow

Sometimes we walked

on the wild side

and grooved to jazz by Kenny G.

We lived in a beige house

and had beige children.

I wish beige was a race

I'm sick of my children

being called out of their name.

She fed me pop tarts

and tuna,

oh I said that already.

She handles my business

You see I play ball.

She and her brothers have turned my cabbage leaves

into a conglomeration of factories.

She was very smart

and suggested I take my name off the deal

to keep the IRS from a piece of the wheel.

She fed me pop tarts

and tuna—

oh there I go, there I go again.

She put my Mother in a nice insurance policy.

Mom soon died

and the conglomeration added a second wing.

We lived happily a lovely life

me kissing her lipless lips

and she being the perfect polyester wife

feeding us pop tarts and tuna.

She did not go to my game one day

said she was sick

With another baby, she thought

for me, of course.

So i left my fellow bulls

and came home early

My poor girl was in bed

with a cold and her french decorator.

All along I thought he was a queer

but there he was using my diamond watch

for a cock ring,

and making my little Nancy sing:

Ooh baby ooh baby

Glory hallelujah.Glory hallelujah.

I hope the bulls go into

overdrive overtime or over whatever

and keep that nigger on the road.

Ooh baby rock me like you ain't

got no back bone.

I stood there for an hour

and watched the frenchman's moon ass

dip baby dip into my pot of gold

before I got my razor

and shaved the shit out of their guts.

My trial was long and

full of difficulty

They cracked my skull

and examined my mentality

Every morning after I shaved

they checked my face for fecal residue.

But my lawyer was slick

and told me to grow a beard.

It came out blond against my black skin.

But I was not alarmed because

married couples do begin to look alike

over time and time again.

Finally the jury set me free

Now I'm on a quest

from east and west.

I must find me a black woman

who's down with cooking

pop tarts and tuna

and a side order of chitlins

if you please.

JUST A LITTLE BIT

Sister, can you spare a cup

of pusseeey?

It's you in the white power suit

I'm talkin' to.

Me—I'm shuffling along in

cardboard shoes.

My anus is caked with

dried sperm.

You see the white man

has been doing me wrong

and doing you right.

I am his enemy

because I am better

better looking and the inventor

of all of his sciences

and if I didn't invent it

it was because I ain't needed to.

A million years ago me and Lucy

learned the moon was an

aphrodisiac—didn't have to go

to the moon to figure that out.

You Sister reinforce my enemy's

notions about himself:

his limp hair is good

his nooses are good for me

'cause I'm a nigga rapist

his children are good

'cause they have this innate desire

to fuck with mars and Venus.

You reinforce his dogma that

country club capitalism

underwritten with tiny print contracts

and reinforced by police

cracking skulls in Watts

and south American jungles

is good for Newark and Nigeria.

You agree with him that I'm ok

when I'm painting a smoky after hours bar

jazzy red and BB king Blue

But leave pork belly futures

and gold speculation to fair haired hero boys

You agree his houses are good

'cause the walls are naked and beige, devoid

of the African triptych

of my black ass, your black ass, Africa's black ass.

He lets you count his money

but under the watchful blue security eye

in case you get the notion to to slip

me a cup of quarters instead of

a cup of . . .

What was it I asked you for?

If a cup full is too much

for you to spare,

then a teaspoon will do

for me to lick.

after all Ronald Reagan

only promised us a trickle

of anything ever now

and then.

About The Author

Charles W. Harvey is a native Houstonian and a graduate of the University of Houston. In 1987, Charles was a 1st place prize recipient of PEN/Discovery for Cheeseburger, which went on to be published in the Ontario Review. In 1989 Charles Harvey was awarded the Cultural Arts Council of Houston Grant for Writers and Artists. Also, in 1989 he was a finalist in the MacDonald's Literary Achievement Awards. Charles has been published in Soulfires, Story Magazine SHADE, High Infidelity, The James White Review, and others. He is the author of the novels The Butterfly Killer, The Road to Astroworld, and Antoine's Double Trouble. He is also the author of several story and poetry collections.

Contact The Author

<u>Facebook</u>[1]

<u>Twitter</u>[2]

<u>WebSite</u>[3]

Illustration*

- The Burning Corpse of William Brown 9/28/1919 Courtesy *Without Sanctuary*

The Publisher and Authors from Wes Writers & Publishers[4] strive to bring you the best in fiction and poetry. We support many fine author/brands and diverse fiction genres. We strive for excellence. A better reading experience won't happen without your valuable input. That's why reviews are so helpful. Please take the time and leave a review. We also want to stay in touch with you. The best way to do so is to join our mailing list. By joining, you will get excerpts from our upcoming titles and other important information about books and publishing. <u>Subscribe</u>[5]

<u>Author's Website</u>[6]

<u>Other Paperback Titles</u>

1. http://on.fb.me/uWapzN

2. https://twitter.com/CharlesHarvey99

3. http://charlesharveyauthor.wordpress.com/

4. http://www.charlesharveyauthor.wordpress.com/

5. https://subscribepage.io/9sPXo5

6. http://charlesharveyauthor.wordpress.com/

When Dogs Bark (The Original Hardcopy)

When Dogs Bark 2 (Later Edition Hardcopy)

Bark Too (Hardcopy)

Americana

Odd Voices in Love (Hardcopy)

Don't miss out!

Visit the website below and you can sign up to receive emails whenever Charles Harvey publishes a new book. There's no charge and no obligation.

https://books2read.com/r/B-A-EWG-TEZ

Did you love *The Last Supper*? Then you should read *Urban Tales*[7] by Charles Harvey!

Discover the captivating world of Urban Tales, where the pulse of city life beats through the pages. These tales are a reflection of the humanity that surrounds us, a celebration of our humor, our loves, our desires, and our secret rendezvous. Only in our urban landscapes could you learn tipping over on the down-low becomes an art form.

In these stories, you'll journey through both the long and the short, the gritty and the heart-touching. Characters come alive through their elegant voices and raw urban tongues, a vibrant fusion of culture and emotion. Brace yourself for the raw truth that might stir discomfort or even bring a tear to your eye, but one thing is for certain - it will never bore you. Urban Tales are an exploration of the human experience, where

7. https://books2read.com/u/3yZNdl

8. https://books2read.com/u/3yZNdl

laughter and love exist alongside the poignant and profound, leaving you with thoughts that linger long after the last page is turned.

Read more at https://charlesharveyauthor.wordpress.com.

Also by Charles Harvey

Astroworld
Promise: Short Stories From The Road to Astroworld
Promise's Letters From the Road to Astroworld

Buck Wile Stories
Buck Wile is Punk'd Out On Da Downlow
Buck Wile is Butt Naked In Da City

Dogs Bark
When Dogs Bark the Short Story
Bark Too

Poetic Journeys
Americana
3AM - Poems and Stories From the Other Mind
The Last Supper
Rough Cut Until I Bleed

Roommates
Roommates and The Old Dead Seaman
Roommates and Other Stories

Standalone
Betty's House
Black Queen
The Blue Train To Heaven
The Power Plant
Ebenezer Jenkins' Christmas in Chicago
Q is a Bad Letter and Other QQ Crazy Stories
Catnip Gray Cat Detective: The Tabitha Davenport Affair
Antoine's Double Trouble
Maura And Her Two Husbands
Urban Tales
Into the Murky Water
David, Jonathan, and Sylvester
Cheeseburger and Other Stories
A Foursome Plus Poems
Kiss and Say Goodbye

Watch for more at https://charlesharveyauthor.wordpress.com.

About the Author

Charles W. Harvey is a native Houstonian and a graduate of the University of Houston. At UofH he studied fiction under the guidance of Rosellen Brown and Chitra Divakaruni. In 1987, Charles was a 1st place prize recipient of PEN/Discovery for his short story Cheeseburger, which went on to be published in the Ontario Review. In 1989 Charles Harvey was awarded the Cultural Arts Council of Houston Grant for Writers and Artists. Also in 1989 he was a finalist in the MacDonald's Literary Achievement Awards. Charles has been published in Soulfires, Story Magazine SHADE, High Infidelity, The James White Review, and others. He is the author of the novels The Butterfly Killer, The Road to Astroworld, and Antoine's Double Trouble. He is also the author of several story and poetry collections. He also writes for the stage and screen.

Read more at https://charlesharveyauthor.wordpress.com.

About the Publisher

Wes Writers and Publishers strives to bring you great books for your reading pleasure. We have been in the business of producing quality works of fiction for over two decades. We will branch out in the future to add more authors to bring you the reader, very high quality and entertaining stories from all genres. It begins with Charles W. Harvey our star prize winning literary writer an poet. He is the author of the prize winning short story Cheeseburger selected by Joyce Carol Oates in the 1987 PEN/Southwest Prize. He is a frequent participant in NANOWRIMO and other literary endeavors. Please feel free to sample his many stories and two Novels via Smashwords and other fine retailers. AC Adams brings you a little something different. He is our premier author for the gay literary erotica genre. Many of our readers have enjoyed his Roommates series. Look forward for a lot more to come from this up and coming author. Clarissa Haley comes from east Texas. She likes quirky little stories that swim around that brain of hers. She has several exciting projects in the works. She has a few romance stories in the works for future release Wes Writers and Publishers (we like being called WWP) will be adding more l writers under its wings in the near future. We love good stories.

Read more at https://charlesharveyauthor.wordpress.com.